EVERYTHING TAYLOR SWIFT
(Gareth's Version)

BY KRISTEN RAJCZAK NELSON

# TAYLOR SWIFT'S MUSIC THROUGH THE ERAS

## COUNTRY DARLING TO GLOBAL SUPERSTAR

Gareth Stevens PUBLISHING

**Please visit our website, www.garethstevens.com. For a free color catalog of all our high-quality books, call toll free 1-800-542-2595 or fax 1-877-542-2596.**

**Library of Congress Cataloging-in-Publication Data**
Names: Rajczak Nelson, Kristen, author.
Title: Taylor Swift's music through the eras : country darling to global superstar / Kristen Rajczak Nelson.
Description: Buffalo, New York : Gareth Stevens Publishing, 2025. | Series: Everything Taylor Swift (Gareth's version) | Includes index.
Identifiers: LCCN 2024025102 | ISBN 9781482469455 (library binding) | ISBN 9781482469448 (paperback) | ISBN 9781482469462 (ebook)
Subjects: LCSH: Swift, Taylor, 1989–Juvenile literature. | Singers–United States–Biography–Juvenile literature. | Country musicians–United States–Biography–Juvenile literature.
Classification: LCC ML3930.S989 R35 2025 | DDC 782.421642092 [B]–dc23/eng/20240610
LC record available at https://lccn.loc.gov/2024025102

Published in 2025 by
**Gareth Stevens Publishing**
2544 Clinton Street
Buffalo, NY 14224



Designer: Tanya Dellaccio Keeney
Editor: Kristen Nelson

Photo credits: cover, (friendship bracelet) Yuliqwiart/Shutterstock.com; Cover (bottom left), 21 Brian Friedman/Shutterstock.com; cover (bottom right), p. 7 (main) Featureflash Photo Agency/Shutterstock.com; cover (left middle) Everett Collection/Shutterstock.com; cover (middle) Raj Valley/Alamy Images; cover (middle right), p. 15 Tinseltown/Shutterstock.com; cover (top left) Ovidiu Hrubaru/Shutterstock.com; cover (top right) a katz/Shutterstock.com; pp. 5 (all), 11, 17 (bottom left), 25 (left) Courtesty of Paolo Villanueva/Flickr.com; p. 7 (banjo) stockphoto-graf/Shutterstock.com; p. 7 (fiddle) TaurusY/Shutterstock.com; p. 8 (mandolin) Gulf MG/Shutterstock.com; p. 9 Patti McConville/Alamy Images; p. 13 landmarkmedia/Shutterstock.com; p. 16 Michael R Helland/Shutterstock.com; p. 17 (top left) https://upload.wikimedia.org/wikipedia/commons/e/e0/Taylor_Swift_-_Reputation_Tour_Seattle_-_Look_What_You_Made_Me_Do_%28cropped%29.jpg; p. 17 (top right) https://upload.wikimedia.org/wikipedia/commons/3/3f/Taylor_Swift_-_Reputation_Tour_Seattle_-_Ready_for_It.jpg; p. 17 (bottom right) https://upload.wikimedia.org/wikipedia/commons/d/db/Taylor_Swift_-_Reputation_Tour_Seattle_-_Getaway_Car.jpg; p. 19 DFree/Shutterstock.com; p. 23 (left) Jordan Strauss/Invision/AP Images; p. 23 (Spotify template) Bagel Studio/Shutterstock.com; p. 23 (folklore album cover) Catrina Haze/shutterstock.com; p. 25 (right) melissamn; p. 26 Hazel Plater/Shutterstock.com; p. 28 (paper) dja-karta/Shutterstock.com; p. 28 (people) Brocreative/Shutterstock.com.



Printed in the United States of America

CPSIA compliance information: Batch #CWGS25: For further information contact Gareth Stevens at 1-800-542-2595.

# CONTENTS



**BOLDFACE** WORDS APPEAR IN THE GLOSSARY.

# MAKING AN ERA

Over Taylor Swift's almost 20 years in the spotlight, she has made music that crosses genres, or kinds of music. She started as a country singer and became a pop music superstar. More recently, some songs feel more like **indie** music than radio hits.

On The Eras Tour, Taylor showcased how her music has changed over time. She **performed** music from each of her albums, calling each an "era." An era is a period of time that has different features than other periods.

**By the end of The Eras Tour, each of Taylor's shows included songs from 11 different "eras" of the albums that she has released, or put out.**

## KNOW IT ALL

Between 2023 and 2024, Taylor put on more than 150 shows in more than 50 cities on The Eras Tour.

# A LITTLE BIT COUNTRY

Taylor started trying to get a record deal in Nashville, Tennessee, around age 11. Nashville was the center of the country-music scene, so it was clear what kind of music she wanted to make.

When *Taylor Swift* came out in 2006, it was a country album. Many songs, including the lead single "Tim McGraw," feature a banjo or fiddle, as well as lots of **acoustic** guitar. Taylor sings about falling in love and the pains of growing up.

KNOW IT ALL

Taylor has a writing credit on every song on *Taylor Swift*. This means she is named as one of the writers of the song. Three songs she wrote entirely by herself: "The Outside," "Our Song," and "Should've Said No."

BANJO

When *Taylor Swift* came out, Taylor was known for her curly blonde hair and often wore cowboy boots.

FIDDLE

# THE FIRST CROSSOVER

When *Fearless* came out in 2008, Taylor was still thought of as a country artist. The popular song "Love Story" featured a country arrangement that included a fiddle, banjo, and mandolin. But it leaned into pop music too! *Fearless* became a huge **crossover** success.

At the 2009 MTV Video Music **Awards**, Taylor won for the best female video. But she was interrupted on stage by rapper Kanye West. This moment and the **feud** that followed would be one cause of Taylor's later reinvention of herself.

MANDOLIN

## IN TAYLOR'S WORDS

"*Fearless* was an album full of magic and curiosity ... It was the diary of the adventures and explorations [of] a teenage girl who was learning tiny lessons with every new crack in the **facade** of the fairy-tale ending she'd been shown in the movies."
(@taylorswift on Instagram, February 11, 2021)

## Country Music Association Award

Album of the Year
2009

## Academy of Country Music Award

Album of the Year
2009

## Grammy Award

Best Country Album
2010

*Fearless* is the most awarded country music album ever. Here are the main awards Taylor won for her work on *Fearless*.

## American Music Award

Favorite Country Album
2009

## Grammy Award

Album of the Year
2010

# A SONGWRITER FIRST

It was important to Taylor to make music she wrote herself. However, because she was a young artist, people wondered how much of her hit songs she had truly written. *Speak Now*, which came out in 2010, answered those questions. Taylor wrote every song on the album without a co-writer.

Though Taylor's star was rising, her music was still thought of as country. She won two Grammy Awards for her work on *Speak Now*, both for country categories, or groupings.

KNOW IT ALL

*Speak Now* sold more than a million copies in its first week.

## *IN TAYLOR'S WORDS*

"A lot of times, I don't know how I feel about something until I write that song about it."
(*Entertainment Tonight*, 2010)

By the *Speak Now* era, everything Taylor did was watched and commented on. She wrote the song "Mean" about a **critic** who wrote unkindly about a live performance she gave.

# MIXING GENRES

The first song released from Taylor's 2012 album *Red,* "We Are Never Ever Getting Back Together," had music critics and fans asking: Was this country music, pop—or something else? Still, the song became Taylor's first number 1 song on the *Billboard* Hot 100 chart. It was also a hit on the country charts!

*Red*'s catchy songs earned Taylor more fans beyond country music. Their pop sound, mixed with other genres, would be a sign of what Taylor's next era would bring.

Taylor changed her look around the time *Red* came out. She cut bangs into her hair and started wearing it straighter. She wore a lot of red, too, including red lipstick.

# THE POP ALBUM

Taylor's next musical era was that of pop superstar! Her album *1989* came out in 2014. The first single was the upbeat "Shake It Off."

Fans new and old loved the range of songs, from the wit and fun of "Blank Space" to the romance, or in-love feeling, of "This Love." In addition, she won the Grammy Award for album of the year. With that, Taylor became the first woman to win that award two times as a solo, or lone, artist.

**KNOW IT ALL**

The 1989 World Tour made the most money of any concert tour in 2015.

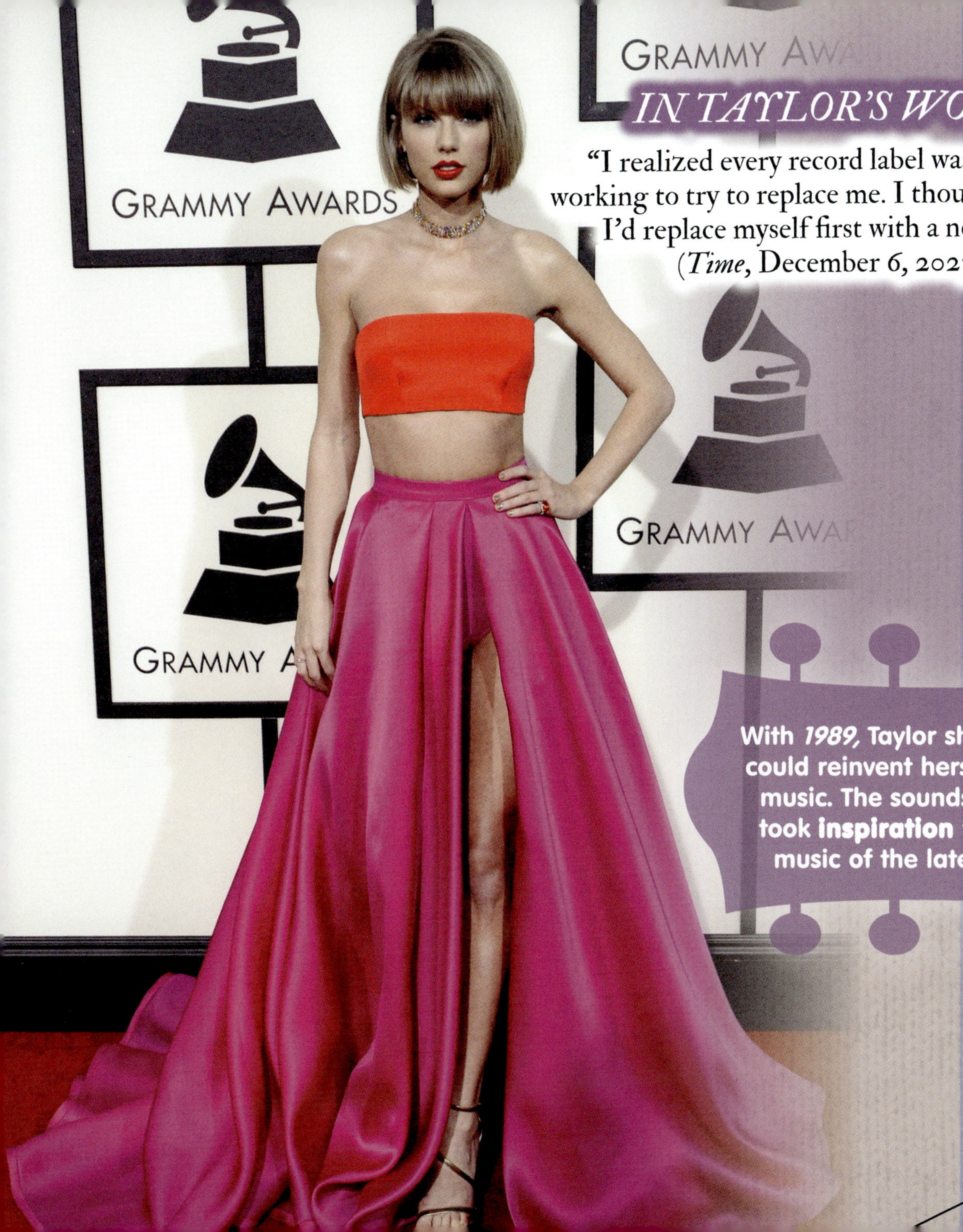


## *IN TAYLOR'S WORDS*

"I realized every record label was actively working to try to replace me. I thought instead, I'd replace myself first with a new me."
(*Time*, December 6, 2023)

With *1989,* Taylor showed she could reinvent herself in her music. The sounds of *1989* took **inspiration** from the music of the late 1980s.

# BAD REPUTATION?

Always being in the spotlight wore on Taylor. This and the ongoing public feud with Kanye West played a part in her break from the public eye between 2016 and 2017.

When ***Reputation*** came out in late 2017, it surprised fans with lots of bass, and songs with a rock and hip-hop feel. Songs about the troubles she had gone through include the lead single, "Look What You Made Me Do." Taylor dressed the part too. It was the era of what many consider her darkest sound—and darkest fashion choices.

**Taylor didn't talk a lot about *Reputation* at the time. However, her lyrics, or the words to her songs, told fans how she felt about what she had gone through.**

AND THEREIN LIES THE ISSUE,
FRIENDS DON'T TRY TO TRICK YOU
GET YOU ON THE PHONE AND MIND-TWIST YOU
AND SO I TOOK AN AXE TO A MENDED FENCE
"THIS IS WHY WE CAN'T HAVE NICE THINGS"

THIS AIN'T FOR THE BEST
MY REPUTATION'S NEVER BEEN WORSE, SO
YOU MUST LIKE ME FOR ME
"DELICATE"

MY CASTLE CRUMBLED OVERNIGHT
I BROUGHT A KNIFE TO A GUNFIGHT
THEY TOOK THE CROWN, BUT IT'S ALRIGHT
ALL THE LIARS ARE CALLING ME ONE
NOBODY'S HEARD FROM ME FOR MONTHS
I'M DOING BETTER THAN I EVER WAS
"CALL IT WHAT YOU WANT"

BUT I GOT SMARTER, I GOT
HARDER IN THE NICK OF TIME
HONEY, I ROSE UP FROM THE
DEAD, I DO IT ALL THE TIME
"LOOK WHAT YOU MADE ME DO"

# SHOWING THE LOVE

*Lover* came out in 2019. Songs like "Paper Rings" and "You Need to Calm Down" returned to the lighter pop sound of *1989*. However, Taylor addressed more adult themes, or ideas, on this album, including **sexism** and her mom's illness.

No one questioned Taylor's music now. In fact, in 2019, the American Music Awards named her the artist of the decade! She performed "Love Story," "Shake It Off," and other hits the night she received the award.

## KNOW IT ALL

Taylor's tour for *Lover* had to be canceled due to the COVID-19 pandemic. A pandemic is a time when a disease, or sickness, spreads quickly and affects a large number of people in a place or throughout the world.

A decade is 10 years. So, naming Taylor the artist of the decade means the American Music Awards thought she was the best or most important artist of the past 10 years!

# MASTERS MESS

*Lover* was Taylor's first album with Republic Records. Her contract with Republic said Taylor would own her master recordings. This was important because she didn't own the masters of her first six albums recorded with Big Machine Records.

Big Machine Records was bought by someone Taylor didn't like in 2019. He sold Taylor's masters again in 2020—even though Taylor wanted to buy them. Still, Taylor had writing credits on all the songs. That meant she could rerecord them after a certain amount of time.

**KNOW IT ALL**

A master recording is the official, original recording of a song. It is sometimes just called a master.

It has always been important to Taylor that she records music she has written. Now, she owns everything she records too!

# SURPRISES IN 2020

Though the pandemic shut down her *Lover* tour, Taylor spent her off time writing music. In 2020, she put out two surprise "sister" albums: *folklore* and *evermore*. The albums were Taylor's first with songs labeled with an E for "explicit." This means the songs have adult language in them.

Both *folklore* and *evermore* had a quieter, more indie sound. Many songs, such as "exile" and "champagne problems" featured Taylor singing over simple piano arrangements. *Folklore* went on to win Taylor her third Grammy for album of the year.

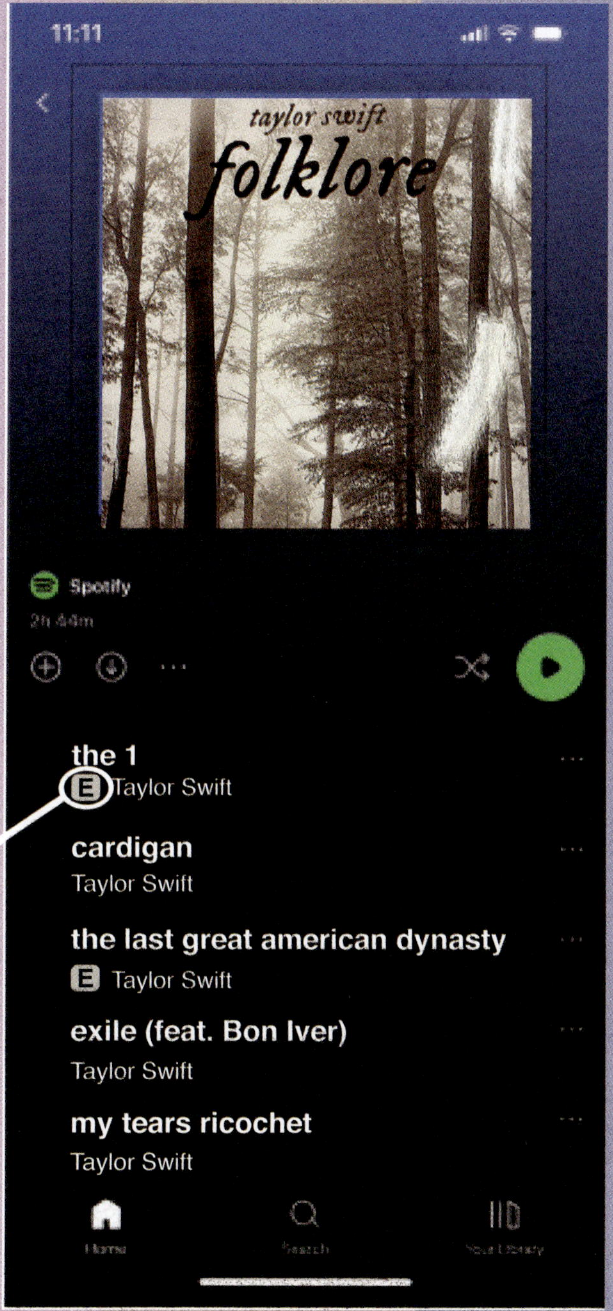


Taylor worked with other musicians to create the indie sounds of *folklore* and *evermore*, including Justin Vernon of Bon Iver and Aaron Dessner of The National.

# WHAT'S OLD IS NEW

In 2021, Taylor put out the first of her rerecorded albums: *Fearless (Taylor's* ***Version****)* and *Red (Taylor's Version)*. She added never-before-heard songs to each and asked fans to buy or listen to the new versions, not the originals.

*Midnights*, an album of new music, came out in 2022. Taylor said it was a collection of songs written throughout her life late at night. It put together the feel of some of her earlier eras including catchy pop choruses, arrangements with heavy bass, and quieter songs.

## IN TAYLOR'S WORDS

"I've always wanted to own my own music since I started making music ... I figured, I was the one who made this music first. I can just make it again. So that's what we're doing. When something says ... 'Taylor's Version' next to it, that means I own it."
(*Late Night with Seth Meyers*, November 12, 2021)

By 2023, Taylor had four albums she had never toured—*Lover, folklore, evermore,* and *Midnights*. They became part of The Eras Tour. Songs from each were featured in the more than three-hour-long show.

# THE NEXT ERA

The Eras Tour became the highest-grossing—or most money-making—tour of all time. Then, in April 2024, Taylor added another era: *The Tortured Poets Department (TTPD)*. The album is a journey through a mix of genres, including the country-inspired "But Daddy I Love Him." Fans loved it. *TTPD* was the first album on Spotify to be streamed more than 300 million times in one day!

A billion-dollar tour, multiple number 1 albums, and hundreds of songs later, and Taylor isn't slowing down. What will her next era be?

***TTPD* hit number 1 on the *Billboard* 200 chart upon its release. It was Taylor's seventh album to sell more than 1 million copies in a week too!**

# TAYLOR'S ALBUMS

2006 Taylor Swift

2008 FEARLESS

2010 Speak Now

2012 RED

2014 1989

2017 reputation

2019 Lover

2020 folklore and evermore

2021 FEARLESS *(Taylor's Version)* and RED *(Taylor's Version)*

2022 Midnights

2023 Speak Now *(Taylor's Version)* and 1989 *(Taylor's Version)*

2024 THE TORTURED POETS DEPARTMENT and
THE TORTURED POETS DEPARTMENT: THE ANTHOLOGY

## *IN TAYLOR'S WORDS*

"There is one thing I've learned: My response to anything that happens, good or bad, is to keep making things. Keep making art."
(*Time*, December 6, 2023)

# COLLAGE ACTIVITY: DEFINE YOUR ERA!

Make a collage to show who you are right now using craft supplies, pictures, magazine clippings, and more! Be sure to ask your caregiver before cutting up pictures and magazines from your home.

## MATERIALS

- poster board
- colored paper
- markers, colored pens, or pencils
- glitter
- paint
- pictures of your friends, family, favorite places, pets, etc.
- magazines
- a phone, tablet, or computer that has internet access (and permission to use it to search for quotes or lyrics)
- glue
- scissors

SO MAKE THE FRIENDSHIP BRACELETS,
TAKE THE MOMENT AND TASTE IT,
YOU'VE GOT NO REASON TO BE AFRAID.
–TAYLOR SWIFT,
"YOU'RE ON YOUR OWN, KID"

# STEPS

## STEP 1

As you gather your supplies, think about the things that make you *you* right now. Make a list! This can include your friend group; your favorite colors, books, movies, and music; the activities you do; and how you feel.

## STEP 2

Look through magazines and find pictures and words that remind you of who you are right now. Cut these out. Do the same thing with pictures.

## STEP 3

Use an internet-connected device to look up quotes you like—and Taylor Swift lyrics! Write these out on your paper or print them out.

## STEP 4

Write, draw, or paint your name on the poster board. Use the colors that define this era of your life! Add glitter, stickers, and more paint if you like.

## STEP 5

Use glue to attach your pictures, words, quotes, and lyrics to the poster board.

## STEP 6

Decorate the collage even more with your other craft supplies.

# GLOSSARY

**acoustic:** Relating to a musical instrument that isn't changed by the use of electrical devices.

**award:** A prize given for doing something.

**critic:** Someone who gives their opinion about music, movies, or other forms of art.

**crossover:** Having to do with gaining success, often because of a shift in musical sound toward more popular styles.

**facade:** The false appearance of something.

**feud:** An ongoing disagreement or argument.

**indie:** Having to do with music not made by a big record company. Also, the sound of this music.

**inspiration:** Something that causes someone to want to do something.

**perform:** To play music or sing.

**reputation:** The views that are held about something or someone.

**sexism:** The unfair treatment of people because of their sex, especially women.

**version:** A form of something that is different from others.

# FOR MORE INFORMATION

## Books

Burk, Rachelle. *The Story of Taylor Swift: An Inspiring Biography for Young Readers*. Naperville, IL: Callisto Publishing, 2024.

Gottlieb, Beth. *Taylor Swift*. Buffalo, NY: Enslow Publishing, 2024.

## Websites

**Taylor Swift**
*www.taylorswift.com/*
Keep up with Taylor on her official website.

**Taylor Swift | Artist | Grammy**
*www.grammy.com/artists/taylor-swift/15450*
Find out more about the Grammy Awards Taylor has been nominated for and won.

**Publisher's note to educators and parents:** Our editors have carefully reviewed these websites to ensure that they are suitable for students. Many websites change frequently, however, and we cannot guarantee that a site's future contents will continue to meet our high standards of quality and educational value. Be advised that students should be closely supervised whenever they access the internet.

# INDEX